"NOTHING WILL EVER REPLACE THE FEELING I GOT WHEN JESSE OROSCO STRUCK OUT MARTY BARRETT....WITHOUT A DOUBT, THAT WAS MY BIGGEST THRILL."

—Gary Carter referring to Game 7 of the 1986 World Series

Stewart, Tabori & Chang
New York

101 Reasons to Love the™

METS

David Green

Introduction

The New York Giants (Gothams at the time) came first, in 1883. Brooklyn's Dodgers were born the following year. The third member of baseball's 20th-century triumvirate, the New York Yankees (Highlanders), did not play their first game until 1903. That was the first year of the modern-day World Series.

Over the next 54 years, preceding the Giants' and Dodgers' moves to the West Coast, at least one of these three teams participated in 33 Fall Classics. And 13 times, the Yankees faced either the Dodgers or the Giants. In short, New York virtually owned major-league baseball in the first half of the 20th century.

But the exodus of the Giants and Dodgers left a gaping hole in the hearts of countless fans and the fabric of New York as a whole. These teams had defined multiple generations and suddenly they were gone, without apology. In 1962, just a few short years removed from arguably the worst moment in New York sports history, the Mets were born.

Can you imagine trying to fill that void? Impossible. Can you imagine trying to field a competitive team patched together from a list of castoffs and has-beens while Mickey Mantle and Roger Maris played a few miles away in the Bronx? Hopeless. At least that's how it had to seem at the time.

And it was bad. So bad it was comedic. Thank goodness the early Mets had such characters as Casey Stengel and Marvelous Marv Throneberry to keep fans interested.

But things changed quickly. The Mets literally won the lottery when the Atlanta Braves botched the signing of a young phenom by the name of Tom Seaver and New York was awarded the opportunity to pick him up. Gil Hodges took over as manager, and suddenly, or so it seemed, the Mets were contenders. When they shocked the world by trouncing the Baltimore Orioles in the 1969 World Series, they owned New York. The Mets, not the Yankees, were world champions.

Hard times returned not long after, but manager Davey Johnson led a resurgence in 1986. The Bad Boys bashed their way to the National League pennant and then staged a miraculous rally to stun the cursed Boston Red Sox for a second World Series title. After nearly 20 years, the Mets once again owned New York.

That pattern has continued. The Yankees continue to win more than their share of championships—and the Mets fall short year after year. The Yankees dominate the sports pages—unless the Mets do something spectacular.

The Mets have often been treated as an afterthought, and worse, in New York—much like Cinderella by her stepsisters. But Cinderella had her day, as did the Mets, and that day will come again.

They may not have the pedigree of the Yanks, but the Mets are just as beloved by their fans. They may be more like a mutt found at your doorstep than a pure-bred that cost a pretty penny, but you love them just the same, maybe more.

The Yankees are easy to love. They win all the time. The Mets are harder to love. They're flawed. They fail much more often than they succeed. They require a deeper, more profound commitment. And that's what makes them special. A Mets fan is a true fan.

LET'S GO METS!

1 The Birth of a Franchise

With New York still mourning the loss of not one but two National League teams in 1958 (the Giants and Dodgers), attorney William A. Shea tried to convince several other teams to relocate to New York. When that didn't work, he petitioned the National League to expand, but the league refused. So Shea decided to form his own, the Continental League, and he hired baseball icon Branch Rickey to run it. With Rickey in charge, the threat of competition became real. Both the American and National Leagues decided to expand. Under the guidance of Rickey, and with the financial backing of Joan Payson, a former minority shareholder of the Giants, Shea was awarded a franchise to be located in New York, and the Mets were born.

Left to right, Mets President George Weiss, NL President Warren Giles, MLB Commissioner Ford Frick, owner Joan Payson, and Mets Chairman M. Donald Grant. Inset, William A. Shea

"BEEN IN THIS GAME 100 YEARS,
BUT I SEE NEW WAYS TO LOSE 'EM
I NEVER KNEW EXISTED."

— Casey Stengel

2 Lovable Losers

How do you spell futility? M E T S. The '62 Mets lineup featured notable veterans Gil Hodges, Richie Ashburn, Frank Thomas, Roger Craig, and Don Zimmer, but their best years were behind them, and the Mets stumbled to a 40–120 finish in their inaugural campaign — the worst record in the modern era. Even with the Old Perfessor, Casey Stengel, at the helm, the team floundered from start to finish, losing their first nine, and 16 of their first 20. The Mets endured losing streaks of 13 and 17 games and never put together a winning streak of more than three games. Craig lost 24 games on the season, and Craig Anderson lost 16 games in a row! Not one to be outdone, Roger Craig proceeded to lose 18 in a row the next year as the Mets finished a miserable 51–111.

Left, 1962 Mets. Right, Roger Craig

3 The Polo Grounds

Unoccupied since 1958, when the Giants left for the West Coast, the Polo Grounds served as home to Casey Stengel's band of lovable losers for two years while Shea Stadium was under construction. The Mets did little to enhance the legacy of the storied ballpark, and after the Mets left, it was demolished to make room for a housing project.

4 The Player to Be Named Later

In April 1962, the Cleveland Indians sent the Mets catcher Harry Chiti for a player to be named later. A few weeks later, the Mets sent Chiti back to Cleveland as said player. The end result? Chiti was traded for himself.

5 What's in a Name?

"Mets" is actually short for Metropolitans, the name of a 19th-century New York ball club that played in the American Association, and also part of the official team name, the New York Metropolitan Baseball Club, Inc. Other nicknames given consideration were Avengers, Burros (a play on the five boroughs of New York), Continentals, Islanders, Jets, Rebels, Skyliners, and Meadowlarks — which was apparently the first choice of owner Joan Payson.

CHITI

6 The Old Perfessor

Casey Stengel, winner of seven World Series as manager of the New York Yankees, was hired to manage and develop the hodgepodge of players that made up the roster of the 1962 Mets. With no free agency at the time, Stengel and President George Weiss had to pick from an assortment of castoffs and has-beens. Stengel was unable to work the same magic on this bunch that he had with the Yankees. His Mets were completely inept, losing 120 games that first year, finishing last, 18 games behind the ninth-place Cubs and an almost unfathomable 60 1/2 games behind the first-place Giants. Things didn't improve much in 1963 or '64. And in 1965, Stengel was forced to retire in mid-season after he fell and broke his hip. He was inducted into the National Baseball Hall of Fame in 1966. Stengel's number, 37, has been retired by the Mets.

"CASEY [STENGEL] KNEW HIS BASEBALL. HE ONLY MADE IT LOOK LIKE HE WAS FOOLING AROUND. HE KNEW EVERY MOVE THAT WAS EVER INVENTED AND SOME THAT WE HAVEN'T EVEN CAUGHT ON TO YET."

— Sparky Anderson

Casey Stengel

7 Stengelese

Casey Stengel was as famous for his commentaries on baseball and his players as he was for his professional success. In regard to the Mets, he offered:

"You look up and down the bench and you have to say to yourself, 'Can't anybody here play this game?'"

"He [Gil Hodges] fields better on one leg than anybody else I got on two."

"We (the Mets) are a much improved ball club, now we lose in extra innings!"

"The Mets are gonna be amazing."

8 Marvelous Marv

Marv Throneberry stumbled his way into the hearts of Mets fans. The career .237 hitter joined the Mets in 1962 and became the poster boy of their futility. He made 17 errors in just 97 games at first base, and countless mistakes on the base paths — including failing to touch either first or second base on his way to a short-lived triple. Still, fans embraced the good-natured Throneberry, facetiously dubbing him "Marvelous Marv."

Marv Throneberry

"HOW COULD HE [THRONEBERRY] BE EXPECTED TO REMEMBER WHERE THE BASES WERE? HE GETS ON SO INFREQUENTLY."

—Jack Lang, sportswriter

9 Coach Upgrade

Casey Stengel was so impressed with San Francisco Giants coach Wes Westrum after meeting him during the 1963 All-Star break that he had the Mets trade first-base coach Cookie Lavagetto to the Giants for Westrum — a rare coach-for-coach trade. Westrum went on to take over for Stengel after Stengel broke his hip in '65, and he led the team to a ninth-place finish in '66 — the first season the Mets didn't finish last and lose more than 100 games.

10 The Orange and Blue

The official Mets colors of orange and blue are a tribute to the two previous National League clubs based in New York, the New York Giants and the Brooklyn Dodgers. The logo includes a skyline that features a church spire, representative of Brooklyn, the borough of churches; the Empire State Building and the United Nations; and a bridge that represents the return of the National League to New York and the team's connection to all five boroughs.

> "BASEBALL IS LIKE A CHURCH. MANY ATTEND BUT FEW UNDERSTAND."
>
> —Wes Westrum

1969 Mets

Pitcher Danny Frisella, left, and bullpen coach Joe Pignatano inspect a tomato plant

11 Old-Timers Day

On July 14, 1962, the Mets held their first Old-Timers Day — a funny thing since they were in their inaugural year and had no Old-Timers. Oh, sure, there were plenty on their active roster, but none who had played for them in years past. Instead, former players of the Brooklyn Dodgers and New York Giants were brought in to play, including Bobby Thomson and Ralph Branca of "The Shot Heard 'Round the World" fame.

12 One Heck of an Exit

Mets catcher Joe Pignatano hit into a triple play in the eighth inning of a 5–1 loss to the Chicago Cubs on the last day of the 1962 season. It was Pignatano's last at bat of his major-league career. Pignatano later redeemed himself as the Mets bullpen coach under Gil Hodges, and by growing an impressive tomato garden in the bullpen.

"WE'VE GOT TO LEARN TO STAY OUT OF TRIPLE PLAYS."

— Casey Stengel

13 Choo Choo

In an interview with Choo Choo Coleman, Ralph Kiner asked, "What's your wife's name and what's she like?" Coleman responded simply, "Her name is Mrs. Coleman and she likes me."

14 Ed Kranepool

No one has played more games in a Mets uniform than Ed Kranepool. Signed right out of James Monroe High School in the Bronx at the age of 17 in 1962, Kranepool went on to become the Mets' everyday first baseman and a fixture in New York for 18 years. In addition to games played, Kranepool is the Mets' all-time leader in at bats, hits, and doubles, and he was part of two pennant winners and the 1969 world-championship team.

15 Running Backward

Talented but mercurial outfielder Jimmy Piersall followed up on his promise by running around the bases backward after hitting his 100th career home run, off Dallas Green of the Philadelphia Phillies on June 23, 1963. The stunt failed to amuse manager Casey Stengel or Mets management, and Piersall was released a month later.

16 "Meet the Mets"

This playful, upbeat anthem by Bill Katz and Ruth Roberts, which debuted back in 1963, is still played during Mets games more than 40 years later.

> "PROBABLY THE BEST THING THAT HAPPENED TO ME WAS GOING NUTS. NOBODY KNEW WHO I WAS UNTIL THAT HAPPENED."
>
> —Jimmy Piersall

Jimmy Piersall trots backward as Phillies catcher Bob Oldis and Tim Harkness look on

17 Shea Stadium

Shea Stadium, named for Mets founder William A. Shea, opened in 1964 in Flushing, Queens. Given the horrible baseball played by the Mets the previous two seasons, it came as no big surprise that New York lost its home opener to the Pittsburgh Pirates, 4–3. On June 21 of the same year, Philadelphia's Jim Bunning pitched the only perfect game in Shea's history, as the Phillies defeated the Mets, 6–0.

But there were also glorious days at Shea, as the Mets captured both of their World Series titles there, in 1969 and 1986. And poignant days, such as when Shea hosted the first game played in New York following the tragic events of September 11, 2001.

In addition to baseball, Shea has hosted the National Football League's New York Jets and Giants, visits from the pope, Beatles concerts, and countless other sports and entertainment events.

The Mets play their final season in Shea in 2008. They will say good-bye to their old friend and move into the new, state-of-the-art Citi Field complex, built just beyond Shea's right-center-field wall, in 2009.

18 The Big Apple

Every time a Mets player hits a home run in Shea Stadium, a giant apple rises out of an inverted "magic" top hat in center field that bears the words "Home Run." Good times.

19 Give Us a Sign

Karl Ehrhardt, aka "the Sign Man of Shea," seemingly had a sign for every occasion. From the time Shea Stadium opened in 1964 until he retired his signs in 1981, Ehrhardt ran a one-man sideshow from his box seats behind the third-base dugout. His black-and-white cardboard signs teased, taunted, and sometimes even inspired. During the horrific early years of the franchise, when M. Donald Grant was team chairman, one of the Sign Man's signs read, "Welcome to Grant's Tomb." But a few short years later, when the Mets stunned the Baltimore Orioles and the world in the 1969 World Series, Ehrhardt hoisted a sign that simply said, "There are no words."

"I JUST CALLED THEM THE WAY I SAW THEM."

—Karl Ehrhardt,
from the *New York Times*

"HE'S SO GOOD THAT BLIND PEOPLE COME TO THE PARK JUST TO HEAR HIM PITCH."

— Reggie Jackson

20 Tom Seaver

Seaver's nickname, "the Franchise," pretty much sums up what he meant to the Mets. He joined the team as a rookie in 1967, winning 16 games and the NL Rookie of the Year award. It only got better from there. From 1968 to 1976, "Tom Terrific" strung together nine consecutive seasons in which he struck out 200 or more batters. Seaver won 25 games in 1969, and the first of his three Cy Young awards, as he led the Miracle Mets to their first world championship. Seaver's 198 wins and 2,541 strikeouts are tops on the Mets' all-time lists.

After a disagreement with Mets chairman M. Donald Grant over his salary, Seaver was traded to Cincinnati on June 15, 1977. The move was devastating to Mets fans and became known as the "Midnight Massacre."

Cincy traded Seaver back to the Mets in late 1982, but he wasn't the same pitcher, and he won just nine games in 34 starts in '83. The Mets left Seaver unprotected in the 1984 free-agent-compensation draft, and the White Sox picked him up. Seaver went on to win his 300th game while pitching for the Sox in Yankee Stadium. He finished with 311 career wins and 3,640 strikeouts. Seaver was a first-ballot inductee into the National Baseball Hall of Fame in 1992. His number, 41, has been retired by the Mets.

21 Almost Perfect

On July 9, 1969, Tom Seaver took a perfect game into the ninth inning against the first-place Chicago Cubs. With one out, Jimmy Qualls blooped a single into left-center field for the Cubs' only hit of the game, ending Seaver's bid for perfection in a 4–0 Mets win at Shea.

Seaver took another no-hitter into the ninth in September 1975, and again it was the Cubs he had handcuffed. But Joe Walls singled with two outs to end the no-hitter, and the Cubs went on to win in 11 innings, 1–0.

22 19 Ks

In a game on April 22, 1970, against San Diego, Tom Seaver struck out 19 batters including the last 10 in a row—a major-league record—as the Mets defeated the Padres, 2–1. According to Jerry Grote, Seaver was so in the zone that Grote quit giving Seaver signs and just let him pitch.

"MY JOB ISN'T TO STRIKE GUYS OUT, IT'S TO GET THEM OUT, SOMETIMES BY STRIKING THEM OUT."

—Tom Seaver

23 The Amazin's

Few, if any, could have predicted the year the Mets would have in 1969 after seven years of perpetual losing. Sure, 1968 had been the Mets' best year to date, but a 73–89 campaign didn't exactly inspire dreams of a world championship. They started slowly, losing seven of their first 10 games, and didn't have a winning record until June 3. But with the young arms of Tom Seaver and Jerry Koosman anchoring a strong pitching staff and manager Gil Hodges at the helm, the Mets suddenly got everyone's attention by winning 20 of 25 from late May into June. They stayed hot, running down the league-leading Chicago Cubs on September 10, sprinting to their first pennant by winning 22 of their last 27 regular-season games, and quickly dispatching the Atlanta Braves, 3 games to none, in the National League Championship Series.

The Mets' World Series opponent, the Baltimore Orioles, fielded a powerful lineup that included sluggers Boog Powell and Frank Robinson, and an outstanding pitching staff that featured Jim Palmer, Mike Cuellar, and Dave McNally. Few gave the Mets much of a chance, and the Orioles easily took the first game, 4–1. The Mets evened the Series in Game 2 as Koosman, with last-out help from Ron Taylor, held the Orioles to one run on two hits. Tommie Agee got the Mets started in Game 3 with a first-inning home run, then made two spectacular catches in the fourth and seventh innings to carry the Mets to a 5–0 win. Seaver got a second chance in Game 4 after his Game 1 loss. He held the Orioles in check and led 1–0 going into the ninth on Donn Clendenon's solo homer in the second, but the Orioles tied it in the ninth on a sacrifice fly by Brooks Robinson. The Mets took a surprising 3-games-to-1 lead in the Series when they scored in the bottom of the 10th to win, 2–1. In Game 5, the Orioles quickly jumped to a 3–0 lead, but the Mets came back to tie the game on homers by Clendenon and Al Weis. New York tacked on two more runs in the seventh on doubles by Cleon Jones and Swoboda. When Jerry Koosman retired the side in the ninth, the Mets had shocked the world.

Ken Boswell

Gil Hodges

Tom Seaver

Tommie Agee

"Tug" McGraw

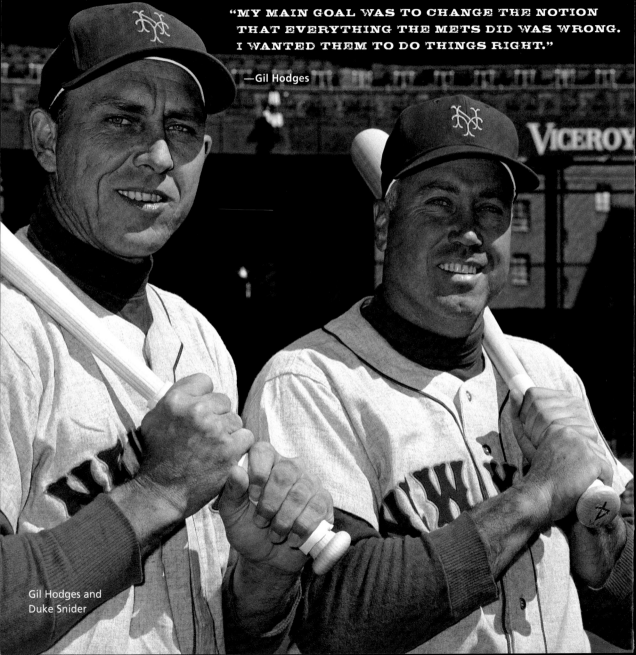

"MY MAIN GOAL WAS TO CHANGE THE NOTION THAT EVERYTHING THE METS DID WAS WRONG. I WANTED THEM TO DO THINGS RIGHT."

—Gil Hodges

Gil Hodges and
Duke Snider

24 Gil Hodges

Hodges, an outstanding first baseman with a big bat, was picked up by the Mets in the 1961 expansion draft, at the tail end of a long career with the Dodgers. Hodges hit the first home run in Mets history on April 11, 1962, in an 11–4 loss to the Cardinals. He was traded the following year to the Washington Senators for Jimmy Piersall, and there he started his managerial career.

The Mets brought Hodges back to New York to manage the team in 1968. Under Hodges, the '68 Mets posted their first season in which they won more than 70 games and lost less than 90. The following year, Hodges guided the Miracle Mets to their first world championship, by beating the powerhouse Baltimore Orioles 4 games to 1 in the World Series. It remains one of the biggest upsets in sports history.

Hodges died tragically, of a massive heart attack, just two days before his 48th birthday in 1972. His number, 14, has been retired by the Mets.

25 Follow Me

Manager Gil Hodges once removed left fielder Cleon Jones in the middle of an inning when Jones made a halfhearted attempt at catching a fly ball in the midst of a 10-run outburst by the Houston Astros. He marched all the way out to Jones, spoke to him briefly, then returned to the dugout with Jones in tow. Hodges sent in Ron Swoboda to finish the game in Jones' place.

GIL HODGES
Manager

METS

26 Donn Clendenon

Tall and powerful, Clendenon was a superb all-around athlete, declining offers to play both professional basketball and football, instead choosing baseball. Originally a star in Pittsburgh, "Big Train" came to the Mets from Montreal during the 1969 season. His big bat helped propel New York to the National League pennant and world championship that year. Clendenon homered in the Mets' 6–0 win over St. Louis that clinched the NL East title. He socked three more round-trippers in the World Series, earning him the MVP award.

27 Cleon Jones

Jones was a key cog in the Mets' miracle season of 1969. He led the team that year with a .340 batting average. Hit by a pitch in the famed "Shoe Polish Incident" in Game 5 of the '69 World Series, Jones started the Mets' comeback that won them their first world championship.

He was part of another huge play in 1973. When Pirate Dave Augustine's apparent home-run ball instead caromed off the top of the wall to Jones, he then fired the ball to third baseman Wayne Garrett. Garrett's relay nailed Richie Zisk at the plate to preserve a 3–3 tie. The Mets went on to win the game, 4–3, in 13 innings to close within a half game of division-leading Pittsburgh, and ultimately they won the National League pennant.

28 The Shoe Polish Incident

In Game 5 of the 1969 World Series, the Mets were trying to close out the Series, but the Baltimore Orioles were not about to go quietly. The Orioles had taken a 3–0 lead in the third inning, and it stayed that way through the middle of the sixth. In the bottom of the inning, a Dave McNally pitch bounced near Cleon Jones' foot. A new ball was put into play, but before play resumed, Gil Hodges came out to argue the call — and he just happened to have a ball that was scuffed with shoe polish as evidence. After some discussion, umpire Lou DiMuro was convinced that Jones had been hit and awarded him first base. Donn Clendenon followed with a two-run homer, and the Mets went on to win the game and their first world championship.

Gil Hodges confers with umpire Lou DiMuro while Cleon Jones and first-base coach Yogi Berra look on

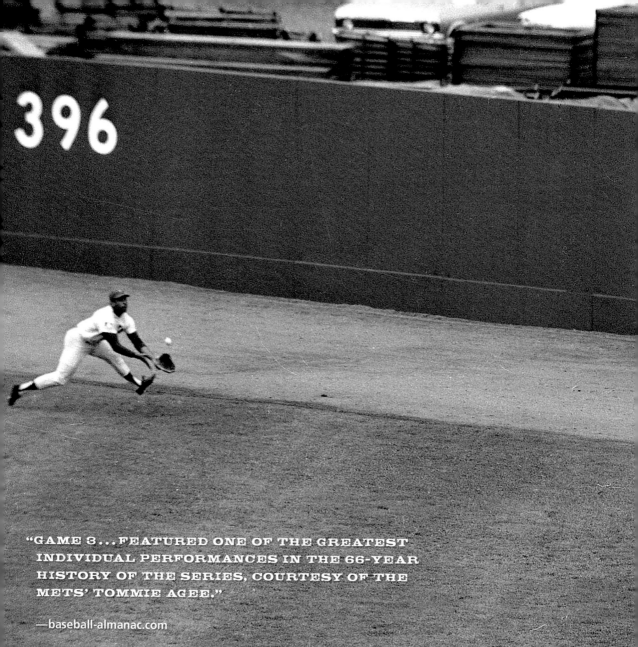

396

"GAME 3...FEATURED ONE OF THE GREATEST INDIVIDUAL PERFORMANCES IN THE 66-YEAR HISTORY OF THE SERIES, COURTESY OF THE METS' TOMMIE AGEE."

—baseball-almanac.com

29 Catching On

In Game 3 of the 1969 World Series versus the Baltimore Orioles, Mets center fielder Tommie Agee made not one but two spectacular catches that almost singlehandedly preserved the Mets' 5–0 win. After hitting a leadoff home run in the bottom of the first, Agee made his first amazing catch in the fourth inning, right in front of the 396-foot sign, snaring Elrod Hendricks' drive and stranding two Orioles runners. In the seventh, with two outs and the bases loaded, Agee saved three more runs when he made a diving grab on the warning track to rob Paul Blair. Both catches have become part of World Series lore.

Not to be outdone, right fielder Ron Swoboda made a remarkable diving grab of Brooks Robinson's liner in the ninth inning of Game 4, saving that game for the Mets.

30 One of a Kind

Tommie Agee's towering blast on April 10, 1969, is still the only home run ever to land in the upper deck of Shea Stadium. His number, 20, marks the spot where the ball landed.

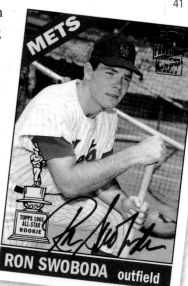

MFTS

RON SWOBODA outfield

Tommie Agee snares Paul Blair's drive as Ron Swoboda looks on, Game 3, 1969

31 The Ryan Express

Worried they might not be able to tame his wildness, the Mets traded Nolan Ryan to the California Angels in 1971 for Jim Fregosi. It's arguably the worst trade in Mets history. Fregosi failed miserably in his new role at third base and was shipped to Texas in 1973. Ryan, in case you don't know, went on to record 324 wins, 5,714 strikeouts, and seven no-hitters in a career that spanned four decades.

32 Kooz

Jerry Koosman won 19 games in his rookie season of 1968. The 19 wins, 2.08 ERA, and seven shutouts are Mets rookie records—even better than Tom Seaver's numbers the previous year. Kooz followed up his rookie campaign with a 17–9 record in 1969. The one-two combination of Seaver and Koosman was hard to beat as the Mets shocked the world that year. Koosman won two games in the World Series—a two-hit masterpiece with reliever Ron Taylor in Game 2, and the Game 5 clincher. He won a career-best 21 games in 1976. Koosman ranks third all-time in wins and strikeouts with the Mets with 140 and 1,799, respectively.

33 Get Outta Here

When the Mets traded Jerry Koosman to the Twins in December 1978, they received reliever Jesse Orosco in return. Koosman threw the last pitch in Game 5 of the Mets' 1969 World Series win over the Baltimore Orioles. Orosco threw the last pitch in the Mets' 1986 World Series win over the Boston Red Sox.

"HE SMART. HE CHANGE SPEEDS.
HE KEEP THE BALL DOWN."

—Camilo Pascual

Jerry Koosman

34 Tug McGraw

Nicknamed Tug by his mother because he used to tug on her when he was breast-feeding, McGraw grew up to become a fan favorite in New York. The bullpen bulldog won nine games and saved 12 in the 1969 champion-ship season, and he posted an ERA of 1.70 in '71 and again in '72, with a career-best 27 saves in '72. McGraw tallied 25 saves in 1973, helping New York win its second NL pennant in five years. Mets fans were heartbroken when he was traded to Philadelphia after the 1974 season.

35 Ya Gotta Believe

In the Mets' run to the 1973 NL pennant, Tug McGraw coined the phrase "Ya gotta believe," which became the team's rallying cry. Apparently, McGraw first chanted it somewhat sarcastically after a pep talk to the last-place squad by team chairman M. Donald Grant, but the phrase caught on and the Mets caught fire.

NY 6 OAK 6   AT BAT BALL STRIKE
               -16   2   1

Yogi Berra trots towards home as Willie
Mays pleads his case to the umpire

36 Yogi

What can you say about Yogi Berra? One of the most beloved players in the history of baseball, Berra was hired as a player-coach by Mets president George Weiss in 1965. Berra played in only four games, but he stayed on as a full-time instructor. When manager Gil Hodges tragically died of a massive heart attack just before the 1972 season was to start, Berra stepped in to manage the team. The Mets started off red-hot under their new leader, but they faded to a third-place finish. The following year, the injury bug bit the team, and they were floundering in last place in mid-August, 13 games under .500. With catcher Jerry Grote and pitcher John Matlack back from injuries, and Tug McGraw rallying the team with his cries of "Ya gotta believe," the Mets surged. After taking four of five games from the Pirates in mid-September, the Mets were tied for first place in the NL's Eastern Division. Yogi's Mets then won five of their last seven to take the division by 1 1/2 games, with a record of 82–79 — the worst ever for a playoff team. No matter: the Mets knocked off the Reds in five games in the NLCS. The mighty Athletics of Oakland finally brought Yogi's Mets back to earth, defeating them 4 games to 3 in the World Series. But with that trip to the Series, Berra became only the second manager, with Joe McCarthy, to manage teams from both leagues in the World Series.

"IT AIN'T OVER 'TIL IT'S OVER."

—Yogi Berra

37 Bud Harrelson

The scrappy shortstop was a fixture on the Mets from 1965 to 1977. Despite a rather weak bat, his stellar fielding and speed on the base paths made him a valuable contributor throughout his career. When Harrelson took exception to Pete Rose's hard slide into second during Game 3 of the 1973 NLCS, the two scuffled and then the benches cleared. Order was eventually restored and the Mets won the game 9–2, then went on to win the series, 3 games to 2. Harrelson had a brief stint as Mets manager in 1990 and '91, but that didn't work out, and he was let go prior to the end of the '91 season.

Bud Harrelson

38 This Rose Smells

After Pete Rose's hard slide into second in Game 3 of the 1973 NLCS initiated a bench-clearing dustup, Shea's faithful showered Rose with an assortment of handy items, including a whiskey bottle, when he took his position in left field. In an effort to quell the unrest and avoid forfeiting the game, Manager Yogi Berra led Mets stars Tom Seaver, Rusty Staub, Cleon Jones, and Willie Mays to the outfield, where they made their appeal for peace. The fans complied and the game was completed. The next day, Rose was the subject of more than a few banners in the stands, including at least one that read, "This Rose Smells."

Pete Rose and Bud Harrelson tangle
during Game 3 of the 1973 NLCS

Willie Mays celebrates winning the 1973 NL pennant. Inset, Rusty Staub

39 Willie Mays

Beloved by New Yorkers from his days as a New York Giant, the "Say Hey Kid" was acquired from the San Francisco Giants in 1972. Mays homered in his first game with the Mets, defeating his old team, 5–4. He tallied 14 of his 660 home runs as a Met and helped them win their second NL pennant in 1973. Mays retired after the '73 season, but he stayed on as a coach with the Mets through 1979.

40 Rusty

Redheaded Rusty Staub was a key player in the Mets' 1973 run to the NL pennant. The gritty outfielder injured his shoulder in the NLCS and was forced to throw underhanded in the World Series matchup with the Oakland Athletics, but he still managed to hit a game-winning home run in Game 4. Staub was traded after the 1975 season, but he returned to New York in 1981 and remained there until he retired in '85. Used primarily as a pinch-hitter in his second stint with the Mets, Staub's home run on September 25, 1984, made him only the second major leaguer, with Ty Cobb, to homer as a teenager and in his 40s.

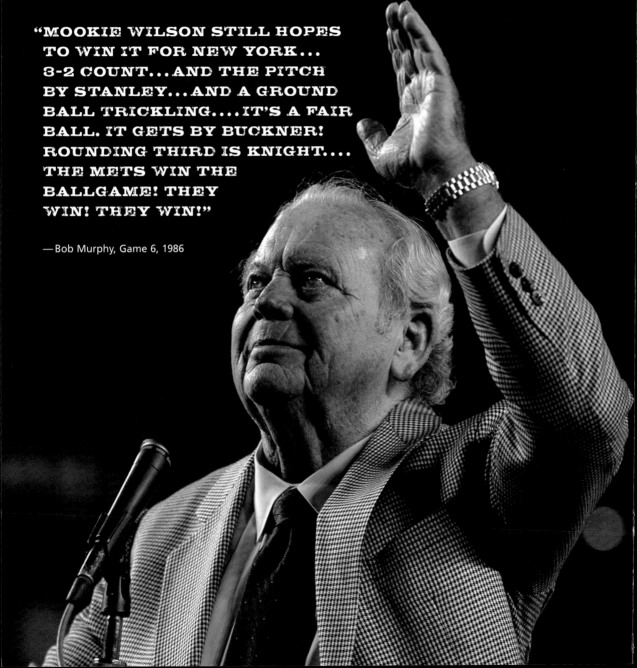

"MOOKIE WILSON STILL HOPES
TO WIN IT FOR NEW YORK...
3-2 COUNT...AND THE PITCH
BY STANLEY...AND A GROUND
BALL TRICKLING....IT'S A FAIR
BALL. IT GETS BY BUCKNER!
ROUNDING THIRD IS KNIGHT....
THE METS WIN THE
BALLGAME! THEY
WIN! THEY WIN!"

—Bob Murphy, Game 6, 1986

41 The Voice of Summer

Smooth and steady Bob Murphy was behind the mike for Mets games for more than 40 years, from the team's inception in 1962 through 2003. Murphy teamed with Ralph Kiner and Lindsey Nelson for many years, telling the tales of ineptitude and glory with style and ease to millions of devoted fans. His call of Mookie Wilson's at bat in Game 6 of the 1986 World Series is perhaps his most memorable. He was inducted into the broadcasting wing of the National Baseball Hall of Fame in 1994.

42 Kiner's Corner

Longtime Mets commentator Ralph Kiner is a master of absurd pronouncements. Some of his best include:

"If Casey Stengel were alive today, he'd be spinning in his grave."

"Solo homers usually come with no one on base."

"There's a lot of heredity in that family."

"All of his saves have come in relief appearances."

"The reason the Mets have played so well at Shea this year is they have the best home record in baseball."

Ralph Kiner

"WHEN YOU SIGN ON
TO DO A JOB, YOU
HOPE YOU'LL BE
ABLE TO GET IT
DONE. BUT THAT'S
NOT ALWAYS IN
YOUR CONTROL."

—Joe Torre

43 Make It a Double

Joe Torre, who would go on to manage the Mets from 1977 to 1981, hit into four consecutive double plays in a 6–2 loss to the Houston Astros in 1975. The Mets teams he managed didn't fare that much better.

44 The Midnight Massacre

It's a defining if not happy moment in Mets history. On the night of June 15, 1977, the Mets did the unthinkable: they traded Tom Seaver to Cincinnati for four young players. Not only that, the Mets also sent slugger Dave Kingman to San Diego for Bobby Valentine, and Mike Phillips was shipped off to St. Louis for Joel Youngblood. The trade of Seaver left a gaping wound that would take years to heal.

45 Oh, God!

In the 1977 smash-hit film *Oh, God!*, starring George Burns as the Almighty, God says to Jerry Landers, played by John Denver, "The last miracle I did was the 1969 Mets. Before that, I think you have to go back to the Red Sea."

46 Chico Escuela

Garret Morris played the heavily accented Hispanic Escuela, sports correspondent for *Saturday Night Live*'s "Weekend Update," during the late 1970s. Escuela, a former Met, had penned a tell-all book on the team entitled *Bad Stuff About the Mets*, which featured such tasty tidbits as "Tom Seaver—he once borrow Chico's soap and no give it back." Escuela became most famous for his oft-repeated line, "Baseball been berry berry good to me."

47 Kong

In his return engage-
ment with the Mets,
Dave Kingman led
the National League
in home runs in
1982 with 37. "Kong"
batted only .204 for
the season. That's the
worst batting average
ever for a home-run
champ.

"NOBODY HITS 'EM FARTHER — OR HIGHER."

—Zander Hollander, *The
Complete Handbook
of Baseball*, 1985

Dave Kingman

48 Travelin' Man

In the dog days of August 1982, Mets outfielder Joel Youngblood went one-for-two off Cubs starter Fergie Jenkins in an afternoon game at Wrigley Field. Informed in the middle of the game that he had been traded to the Montreal Expos, Youngblood packed up and flew to join his new team in Philadelphia, where he singled off Phillies starter Steve Carlton. Youngblood became the first major leaguer ever to get hits for two different teams in two different cities on the same day.

49 Great Names

Benny Agbayani, Billy Beane, Yogi Berra, Rico Brogna, Buzz Capra, Duke Carmel, Elio Chacon, Choo Choo Coleman, Octavio Dotel, D. J. Dozier, Duffy Dyer, Jorge Fabregas, Bartolome Fortunato, Brent Gaff, Pumpsie Green, Butch Huskey, Jorge Julio, Takashi Kashiwada, Lou Klimchock, Satoru Komiyama, Clem Labine, Hobie Landrith, Vinegar Bend Mizell, Xavier Nady, Amos Otis, Desi Relaford, Mackey Sasser, Al Schmelz, Esix Snead, and Turk Wendell.

Joel Youngblood

Neil Allen

50 Finishing Up

Eccentric reliever Neil Allen was once found sitting at manager George Bamberger's desk in the clubhouse munching on a hamburger during a game. What made this particularly egregious was that pitching coach Bill Monbouquette had called down to the bullpen to have Allen start warming up.

51 Sidd Finch

George Plimpton penned an article on Finch for *Sports Illustrated*'s April 1, 1985, issue. Supposedly Finch was at the Mets' spring-training complex in St. Petersburg, Florida, and the heretofore unheard-of rookie could throw a baseball 168 miles per hour with incredible accuracy. Finch pitched with a hiking boot on his right foot and a bare left foot. His catcher described his motion as "a pretzel gone loony." Raised in an orphanage, and later a student at Harvard and then a monastery in Tibet, Finch was also considering pursuing a career as a French horn player. The story generated incredible interest, but it was subsequently revealed to be an April Fools' Day hoax. Plimpton later expanded the story into a novel.

52 Fireworks Night

July 4, 1985, was Fireworks Night at Atlanta's Fulton County Stadium. The show was set to start immediately following the Braves' game with the Mets. The only problem was that the game endured two rain delays and more than six hours of playing time. It went 19 innings and didn't end until 3:55 in the morning. Not wanting to renege on their promise, Braves officials decided to go on with the show. So, at 4:01 a.m., much to the surprise of slumbering local residents, fireworks lit up the Atlanta sky.

53 Bunnyball

Baseball franchises are forever coming up with new and wacky promotions to fill the seats. Among the most "innovative" promotions Mets marketing came up with was a softball game featuring Playboy bunnies, ironically benefiting the Lighthouse for the Blind.

"IF YOU CAN GET AN OUT
ON ONE PITCH, TAKE IT."

—Dwight Gooden

54 Dwight Gooden

Overpowering. That's the best way to describe "Doc" Gooden in his early years. In 1984, Gooden tied Jerry Koosman's Mets rookie record with 17 wins, and he was given the NL Rookie of the Year award. Only 20 years old when the season ended, Gooden had 276 strikeouts in only 218 innings pitched, setting a major-league rookie record. Gooden was even more dominating in his sophomore season. He led the National League in wins (24), ERA (1.53), strikeouts (268), and complete games (16), winning the Cy Young award. In the championship season of 1986, Gooden posted 17 regular-season wins, and he pitched two superb games in the NLCS. He took a tough-luck, 1–0 loss to the Astros and Mike Scott in Game 1. In Game 5,

Gooden gave up only one run in 10 innings, but he had a no-decision in the Mets' 12-inning win. Injuries took their toll on Gooden in the ensuing years. Drug problems resulted in his one-year suspension from baseball in 1995, and the end of his tenure with the Mets. In 11 years in orange and blue, Gooden's 157 wins and 1,875 strikeouts are second only to Tom Seaver's totals.

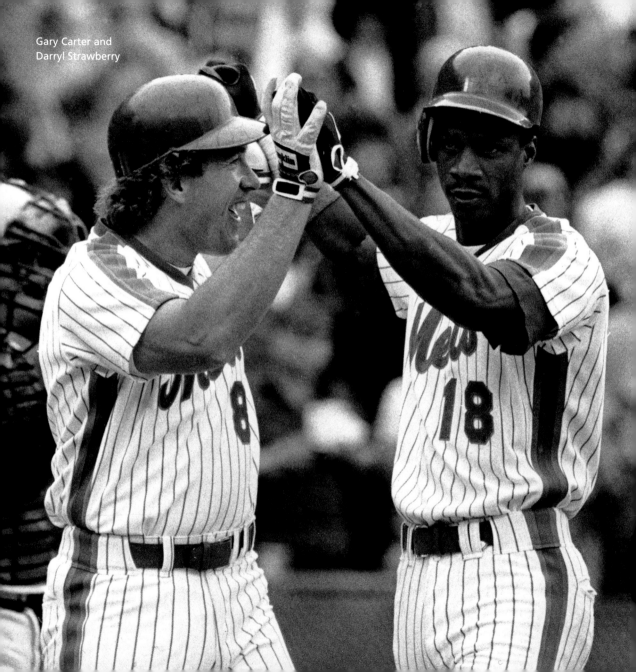

Gary Carter and
Darryl Strawberry

55 Darryl Strawberry

The Straw Man was at the center of the power lineups the Mets fielded during the 1980s. Strawberry won the NL Rookie of the Year award in 1983 following a 26-home-run, 74-RBI season. Each of those totals was the fewest he would tally in eight years with the Mets, racking up 39 homers in 1987 and '88, and topping 100 RBI in both campaigns. Like Doc Gooden, Strawberry succumbed to the temptations of money and fame, which ruined a promising career. Still, Strawberry is the Mets' all-time leader in home runs and RBI with 252 and 733, respectively.

56 Ho-Jo

Howard Johnson, who shares his name with the once ubiquitous orange-roofed motel chain, was a star in orange and blue. Ho-Jo joined the Mets in 1985, platooning with Ray Knight at third base and also playing some shortstop and outfield. He quickly became an offensive force for the Mets, putting together three seasons of 30-plus home runs, including two, 1987 and '89, in which he also stole more than 30 bases, making him only the third player ever to have two 30–30 seasons. Johnson is the only Met to lead the league in two Triple Crown categories in the same season, with 38 home runs and 117 RBI in 1991.

Howard Johnson

57 Jesse Orosco

Orosco's best year with the Mets statistically was 1983, when he won 13 games, saved 17 more, and posted a 1.47 ERA. But what he's really remembered for is his three wins in the 1986 NLCS versus Houston, including a game-saving strikeout of Kevin Bass in the Game 6 clincher, and his two saves in the World Series, the second coming in Game 7 as the Mets won their second world championship. In all, Orosco spent 24 seasons in the majors—eight with the Mets—and he's the all-time major-league leader in appearances with 1,251.

58 The Prankster

Roger McDowell teamed with Jesse Orosco to share the Mets' closer role during their run to the 1986 world championship. The notorious prankster kept teammates loose with all sorts of antics, including once wearing his uniform upside down with his pants on his head.

Roger McDowell

Right, 1986 All-Stars Dwight Gooden, Jesse Orosco, and Keith Hernandez

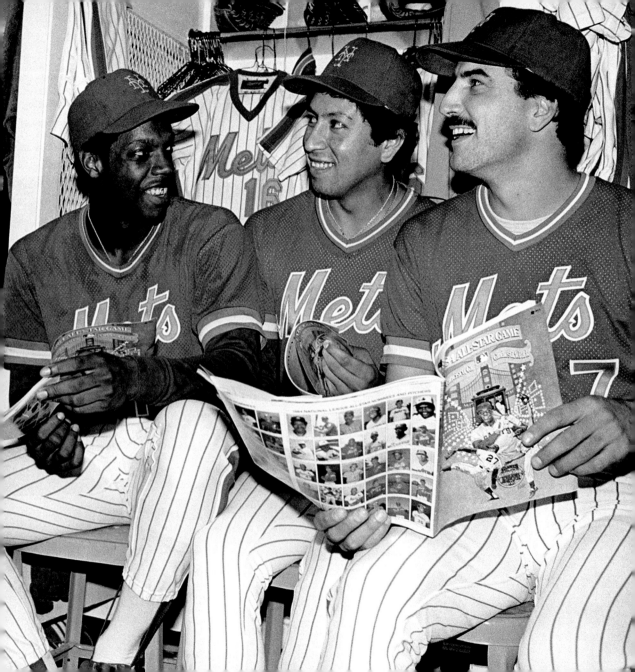

59 The Kid

Gary Carter came to the Mets in an off-season trade with the Expos between the 1984 and '85 seasons. The gritty, gung-ho, All-Star catcher was a key acquisition for the rebuilding franchise. His management of the young pitching staff was masterful, and his unbridled enthusiasm was infectious. The Kid immediately let everyone know he came to play, launching a game-winning homer on opening day, 1985. Carter smacked three consecutive home runs in a game later that year, and he poked two more in Game 4 of the '86 World Series. His biggest hit, however, may have been the two-out, 10th-inning single in Game 6 that started the Mets' unforgettable rally. Carter was inducted into the Hall of Fame in 2003.

"I'VE HAD NINE KNEE SURGERIES. I'VE HAD A COUPLE OF BROKEN THUMBS, ONE ON EACH HAND. I CAN LOOK BACK AT IT AND SAY IT'S WORTH IT."
—Gary Carter

Gary Carter tags out Jim Rice in World Series Game 6, 1986

Lenny Dykstra rounds the bases after his leadoff
home run in Game 3 of the 1986 World Series

60 Nails

"Tough as nails" described Lenny Dykstra perfectly. Dykstra knew only one way to play the game, and that was full throttle all the time. His aggressive fielding made for some memorable catches in center field, and his timely hitting helped ignite a powerful Mets offense. "Nails" won Game 3 of the 1986 NLCS with his two-run ninth-inning homer, and he jump-started the Mets offense in Game 3 of the World Series with his leadoff blast in Boston's Fenway Park. Dykstra played only 4 1/2 seasons in New York before he was shipped to Philadelphia in 1989, along with reliever Roger McDowell, in the infamous Juan Samuel trade.

61 Marry Me

During the Mets' championship season of 1986, a young woman showed up at several Mets games wearing a wedding dress and carrying a sign that said, "Marry Me, Lenny," in reference to gritty center fielder Lenny Dykstra. The young lady even traveled to Chicago's Wrigley Field in her attempt to persuade the already hitched Dykstra.

Gary Carter, 1986 NLCS

62 Working Overtime

The Mets motored through the 1986 regular season, winning a team-record 108 games, but the Houston Astros proved to be one tough opponent in the NLCS. The teams split the first four games, with Houston's Mike Scott shutting down the high-powered Mets offense in Games 1 and 4. Nolan Ryan and Doc Gooden staged a pitcher's duel in Game 5 that went to the 12th inning tied at 1. Gary Carter won it for the Mets in the bottom of the 12th with an RBI single.

Game 6 became an instant classic. The Astros jumped out to a 3–0 lead in the first. The score held into the ninth, and the Mets faced the specter of Mike Scott in a Game 7 matchup for the NL pennant. Lenny Dykstra got things started in the top of the ninth with a triple. Mookie Wilson's single, Keith Hernandez' double, two walks, and a sacrifice fly by Ray Knight tied the game, and it remained that way through the 13th. The Mets took a one-run lead in the 14th on Wally Backman's RBI single. Houston tied the game again in the bottom of the inning on Billy Hatcher's home run off the foul-pole screen. The Mets seemed to lock up the game and the series in the 16th, when they scored three runs. But the Astros rallied to score two off Jesse Orosco and had a chance to win the game with two on and Kevin Bass at the plate. After a conference on the mound with Carter and Hernandez, in which Hernandez not-so-subtly told Orosco to lay off the fastballs, Orosco struck out Bass to end the game and send the Mets to their first World Series since 1973.

Jesse Orosco

63 "If You Throw One More Fastball...

we're gonna fight." That was Keith Hernandez' "advice" to Jesse Orosco in the bottom of the 16th in Game 6 of the 1986 NLCS, with the Mets clinging to a one-run lead and two Astros on base. Orosco snuck a slider past Kevin Bass to strike him out and give the Mets the NL pennant.

64 Keith Hernandez

A mid-season trade with St. Louis brought "Mex" to the Mets in 1983 for pitchers Neil Allen and Rick Ownbey. It turned out to be one of the best trades in Mets history. Hernandez was one of the game's all-time great first basemen and a terrific hitter, compiling 11 consecutive Gold Glove seasons and sharing the '79 NL MVP award with Willie Stargell. Something of a problem child with St. Louis, Hernandez cleaned up his act in New York and became a team leader and key ingredient in the championship year of 1986. He hit better than .300 in each of his first three seasons in New York and drove in more than 80 runs for four straight years. Hernandez is currently a member of the Mets' broadcast team.

65 The Boyfriend

Keith Hernandez played himself in two 1992 episodes of the hit television comedy *Seinfeld*. In the shows, Hernandez dates Seinfeld's former girlfriend Elaine, while Jerry's neighbors, Kramer and Newman, accuse Hernandez of spitting on them following a Mets loss. The story features the "Magic Loogie" sequence, which satirically parallels the Oliver Stone movie *JFK* and the conspiracy theories surrounding the assassination of John Kennedy. Jerry ultimately determines that there was a "second spitter"—Mets reliever Roger McDowell.

"YOU CAN GET CAUGHT UP IN YOUR OWN STATISTICS AND GET YOURSELF IN A LOT OF TROUBLE. IT'S A LONG SEASON."

—Keith Hernandez

66 Rounding Third Is Knight

Just about everyone knows the story by now. 1986. The Mets trailed the Red Sox 3 games to 2 in the World Series and faced a two-run deficit in the bottom of the 10th inning in Game 6. New York was down to its last out. Gary Carter singled. Then Kevin Mitchell singled. Suddenly there was life in Shea Stadium. Red Sox reliever Calvin Schiraldi, a former Met, got two strikes on Ray Knight. The Mets were one strike away from oblivion. Knight fought off Schiraldi's inside fastball, and his broken-bat single scored Carter as Mitchell advanced to third. Bob Stanley replaced Schiraldi and got two quick strikes on Mookie Wilson. With the count at 2–2, Wilson fouled off two pitches to stay alive. Stanley's next offering skipped past catcher Rich Gedman, and Kevin Mitchell came in to score the tying run. With Ray Knight on second, Wilson spoiled two more pitches before topping a roller down the first-base line. The ball squirted between first baseman Bill Buckner's legs, Knight scored from second, and the Mets had miraculously won Game 6. In Game 7, the Mets trailed 3–0 early, but they came back to top the Sox, 8–5, and win their second World Series title.

Michael Sergio parachutes into Shea Stadium during Game 6 of the 1986 World Series

67 Mookie

One at bat defines Mookie Wilson's legacy with the Mets. A fan favorite for his hustling style, Wilson was at the plate in the bottom of the 10th inning of Game 6 of the 1986 World Series, with the Series on the line. With two on, two outs, and two runs already in, Wilson's squibber down the first-base line got past first baseman Bill Buckner, Ray Knight scored, and the rest is history.

68 Free Sergio

In the top of the first inning of Game 6 of the 1986 World Series, with the Boston Red Sox leading the Series 3 games to 2 and looking to end 68 years of frustration with a victory, Michael Sergio dropped from the sky underneath a billowing parachute. Clad in a white jumpsuit and trailed by a banner that read, "Go Mets," the soap-opera actor parachuted onto the infield grass, only to be quickly escorted away by security. He later served 21 days in jail for refusing to reveal the name of the pilot who had aided his jump, prompting a plea at Banner Day the next year that read, "Free Sergio."

"ONCE YOU START WINNING...
YOU DON'T WANT TO STOP.
YOU DON'T WANT TO LOSE."

—Davey Johnson

Davey Johnson and Lenny Dykstra

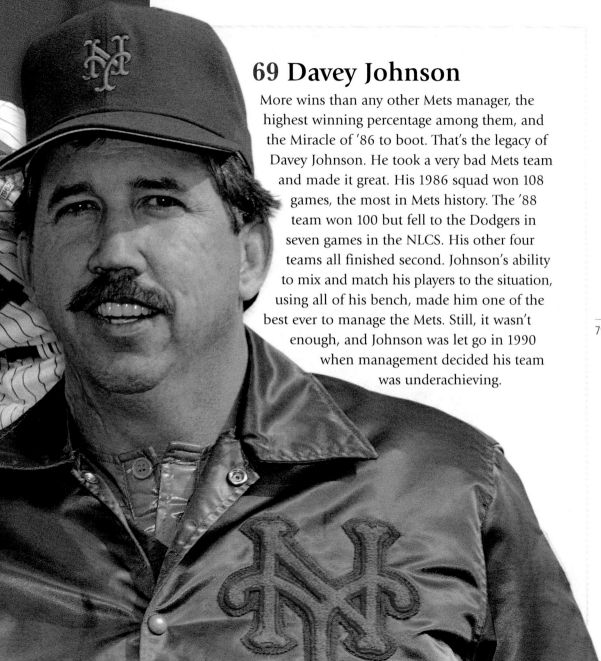

69 Davey Johnson

More wins than any other Mets manager, the highest winning percentage among them, and the Miracle of '86 to boot. That's the legacy of Davey Johnson. He took a very bad Mets team and made it great. His 1986 squad won 108 games, the most in Mets history. The '88 team won 100 but fell to the Dodgers in seven games in the NLCS. His other four teams all finished second. Johnson's ability to mix and match his players to the situation, using all of his bench, made him one of the best ever to manage the Mets. Still, it wasn't enough, and Johnson was let go in 1990 when management decided his team was underachieving.

Rafael Santana removes bird killed
by Dion James' pop fly. James stands
at second base with a double.

70 Double Trouble

Atlanta Braves outfielder Dion James got a little help from above when his routine fly ball collided with a suicidal pigeon in an April 12, 1987, contest with the Mets at Shea Stadium. The pigeon's deflection allowed the ball to drop uncaught, and James ended up at second with a double. Neither the Mets nor the pigeon recovered, as the Braves went on to win the game, 12–4.

71 Johnny Be Good

A fixture in New York for 14 seasons, John Franco grew up in the Bensonhurst section of Brooklyn, idolizing Mets legend Tug McGraw. The Mets acquired Franco for Randy Myers after the 1989 season, in a rare exchange of closers. He's the all-time leader in saves for the Mets with 276, and is fourth all-time in the major leagues with 424, trailing only Trevor Hoffman, Lee Smith, and Mariano Rivera. The homegrown fan favorite made the trek from bullpen to mound to the blaring chorus of Chuck Berry's "Johnny Be Good."

John Franco

72 Show Me the Money

In a passionate show of frustration at the Mets' 1992 team of over-paid underachievers, a disgruntled fan ran onto the field sporting a T-shirt with the word "Greed" inscribed in large capital letters. The fan directed his abuse at Bobby Bonilla, who stood with his arms crossed as the fan flung dollar bills at him. Bonilla, by the way, had more strikeouts (73) than RBI (70) on the year and hit only .249.

73 Don't Walk

Bret Saberhagen accomplished a rare feat for the Mets in 1994. He had more wins (14) than batters walked (13). You have to go back to 1919 to find the previous pitcher to accomplish this — Cincinnati's Slim Sallee.

74 A Young 27

From May 6, 1992, to July 24, 1993, Mets reliever and occasional starter Anthony Young strung together a major-league-record streak of 27 consecutive losses. Young finally broke the streak four days later when the Mets topped the Florida Marlins, 5–4, with two runs in the bottom of the ninth, after Young had allowed the go-ahead run in the top of the inning.

Anthony Young

Bret Saberhagen

David Cone

75 19 Ks, Take 2

David Cone matched Tom Seaver's team and National League record by fanning 19 Phillies in the 1991 season finale in Philadelphia. (The NL record was broken by Chicago's Kerry Wood in 1998.) Cone held the Phils to three hits in a 7–0 Mets victory. He won 80 games in 5 1/2 seasons with the Mets, including a 20–3 record in 1988.

76 Ladies' Day

With the players' strike of 1994 still unresolved as the 1995 season approached, the Mets offered tryouts during spring training to pitcher Ann Williams and infielder Shannan Mitchem, members of the Colorado Silver Bullets, an all-female, traveling team. Both were released, though Mitchem did make the first cut. Wonder what their baseball cards would be worth had they made the squad?

Shannan Mitchem

Dave Mlicki, 1997
interleague game

10:19 OFFICIAL TIME

Armitron

	1	2	3	4	5	6	7	8	9	10	R	H	E
METS	3	0	0		0	0	0		2	0	1	6	9	2
YANKEES| 0	0	0		0	0	0		0	0		0	9	1

REAL BREWED ICED TEA

Coca-Cola

Bell Atlantic
NYNEX

77 Dave's Day

In the very first interleague contest between the Mets and Yankees in 1997, Mets right-hander Dave Mlicki shut down the world-champion Bronx Bombers, tossing a complete-game shutout in a 6–0 Mets win. It was the first complete game and shutout of his career.

78 Something Wild

The Mets and Cincinnati Reds finished the 1999 regular season in a dead heat with identical 96–66 records. They met on October 4 to determine the National League's wild-card team. Al Leiter pitched a complete-game, two-hit gem as the Mets thumped the Reds, 5–0, and moved on to the Division Series, their first playoff appearance in 11 years.

79 The Infield

First baseman John Olerud set the Mets' record for highest batting average in a season with a mark of .354 in 1998. He combined with the rest of the 1999 Mets infield—Robin Ventura, Rey Ordoñez, and Edgardo Alfonzo—to make only 27 errors over the course of the entire year, making them one of the best defensive infields in major-league history.

John Olerud

Al Leiter

80 Razing Arizona

Building on Al Leiter's inspired performance in the wild-card playoff with Cincinnati, the Mets roared into Arizona to face the Diamondbacks in the 1999 Division Series. Edgardo Alfonzo got things started in Game 1 with a ninth-inning grand slam, his second homer of the game, and Todd Pratt finished off Arizona with a series-ending walk-off homer in Game 4 that just eluded Steve Finley's grasp above the center-field wall. Pratt's blast was just the fourth series-ending home run in post-season history.

81 Fonzie

Edgardo Alfonzo's two-out, ninth-inning grand slam vaulted the Mets past Arizona in Game 1 of the 1999 NLDS, 8–4. "Fonzie" had an even more impressive night on August 30 of that same year. Fonzie went 6-for-6, with three home runs, five RBI, and six runs scored. In eight years with the Mets, the slick-fielding Alfonzo hit better than .300 four times, including a career-high .324 in the pennant year of 2000.

82 Ventura's Slam

After all the fireworks in the 1999 NLDS, the Mets fizzled as they opened the National League Championship Series versus the Atlanta Braves. Atlanta won the first three games of the series, and they stood one win away from a sweep when the Mets stole Game 4 with a two-run rally in the ninth. Game 5 was tied 2–2 after nine, as a steady rain fell at Shea. The battle continued into the 15th inning, when the Braves plated a run for a 3–2 lead. The Mets faced elimination if they couldn't squeeze a run across in the bottom of the frame. An intentional walk to John Olerud loaded the bases for the Mets, and when Todd Pratt coaxed another walk, the game was once again tied. Up came Robin Ventura with a chance to keep the Mets' season alive. Ventura launched a shot to right field that just managed to clear the fence for a game-ending grand slam — except that the Mets players were so excited they mobbed him between first and second base, and Ventura never made his way to home. His blast was later ruled a single, and it became known as "the grand-slam single." Unfortunately, the Braves finished off the Mets in Game 6, when Kenny Rogers walked in the winning run in the bottom of the 11th inning.

Teammates mob Robin Ventura after his game-winning "grand-slam single"

Bobby Valentine
expresses his
views to umpire
Ed Rapuano

83 Bobby V

Bobby Valentine wore his heart on his sleeve. He wasn't afraid to speak his mind. These traits made him able to take some of the focus off his players during tough times, but his outspokenness didn't always sit well with everyone in the clubhouse, or in the front office. Valentine took over for Dallas Green as manager of the Mets near the end of the 1996 season. His squads won 88 games in each of the next two years, and 97 in 1999, which earned the Mets a spot in the post-season as the NL wild card. They fell to the Braves in six games in the NLCS. In 2000, the Mets again finished second in the NL East, but this time they knocked off the Cardinals in the NLCS to advance to the World Series, where the crosstown Yankees defeated them in five games. When the Mets failed to make the playoffs the following two years, Valentine was relieved of his duties.

84 Master of Disguise

Following his ejection from a June 1999 game, and mandatory evacuation from the dugout, manager Bobby Valentine went into the clubhouse, changed clothes, applied eye-black patches as a mustache, put on sunglasses, and returned to the dugout incognito — or so he thought. He was caught on camera, and the League saw fit to punish Valentine's charade by fining him $5,000 and suspending him for two games.

"I'VE NEVER CRITICIZED MY PLAYERS IN PUBLIC, AND I'LL NEVER DO IT AGAIN."

— Bobby Valentine

85 A Ten-Spot

In the summer of 2000, the Mets overcame an eighth-inning 8–1 deficit to the Braves, scoring 10 runs in the inning, nine of them with two outs. Mike Piazza's three-run homer was the game winner in the 11–8 Mets victory.

86 Slaying the Giants

In another classic clutch performance by a Mets pitcher, New York defeated San Francisco 4–0 behind Bobby Jones' one-hitter in Game 4 of the 2000 NLDS. Robin Ventura homered as the Mets finished off the Giants, 3 games to 1.

87 The Wild Man

Mention the name Armando Benitez to Mets fans, and you may elicit a wry grin— or you may see a grimace. Benitez was the Mets' closer from 1999 to 2003, taking over after John Franco was injured. Known as much, if not more, for his spectacular meltdowns as for his overpowering fastball, Benitez proceeded to rack up 160 saves in his tenure with the Mets, including a club-record 43 in 2001. But his complete lack of consistency led to his dismissal in 2003.

"I FEEL REALLY COMFORTABLE AND CONFIDENT THAT I CAN DO MY JOB."

—Armando Benitez

Armando Benitez

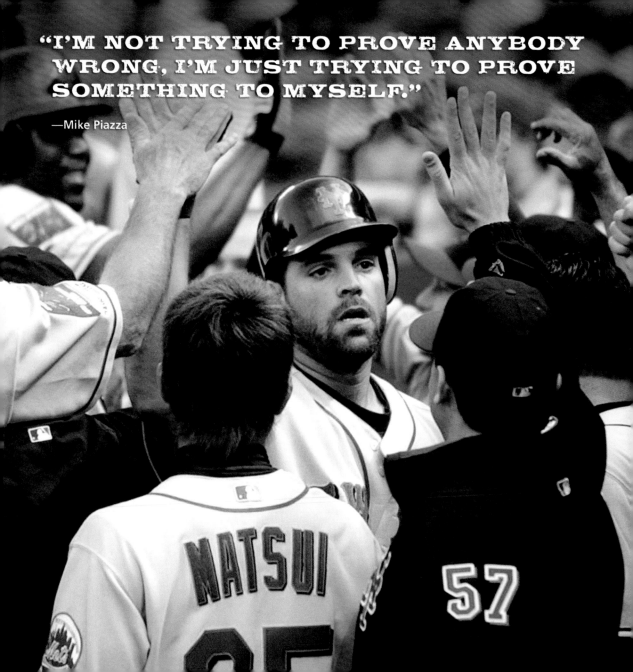

"I'M NOT TRYING TO PROVE ANYBODY WRONG, I'M JUST TRYING TO PROVE SOMETHING TO MYSELF."

—Mike Piazza

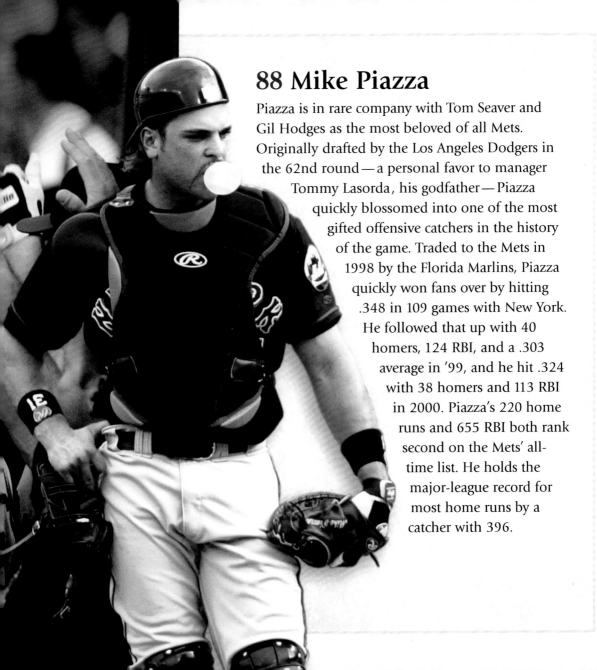

88 Mike Piazza

Piazza is in rare company with Tom Seaver and Gil Hodges as the most beloved of all Mets. Originally drafted by the Los Angeles Dodgers in the 62nd round—a personal favor to manager Tommy Lasorda, his godfather—Piazza quickly blossomed into one of the most gifted offensive catchers in the history of the game. Traded to the Mets in 1998 by the Florida Marlins, Piazza quickly won fans over by hitting .348 in 109 games with New York. He followed that up with 40 homers, 124 RBI, and a .303 average in '99, and he hit .324 with 38 homers and 113 RBI in 2000. Piazza's 220 home runs and 655 RBI both rank second on the Mets' all-time list. He holds the major-league record for most home runs by a catcher with 396.

89 The Subway Series

First, the wild-card Mets of 2000 knocked off the Giants in the NL Division Series with Bobby Jones and Benny Agbayani playing the heroes. Mike Hampton and Todd Zeile led the charge past the Cardinals in the NLCS. With the pennant came the first Subway Series in 44 years, as the Mets faced the Yankees in the battle of the Big Apple. The Mets took a 3–2 lead in the seventh inning of Game 1, only to have Armando Benitez blow the save in the bottom of the ninth. The Yanks went on to win the game, 4–3, in 12 innings. It was all Yanks in Game 2, until the top of the ninth. The Mets scored five runs to cut the six-run margin to one, putting a scare into the Yanks, but still falling short. The Mets won the Game 3 battle at Shea, 4–2, with two runs in the eighth. Yankees shortstop Derek Jeter lined Denny Neagle's first pitch into the seats to start Game 4, and the Yanks went on to a 3–2 win. Two runs in the ninth gave the Yanks a 4–2 win in Game 5, and the Mets' dreams of a third world championship, at the expense of the Yankees, died.

90 A Night to Remember

In the aftermath of the tragic events of September 11, 2001, major league baseball was postponed for a week. When it resumed, the Mets swept a three-game set in Pittsburgh before returning home to face the Atlanta Braves, in the first major sporting event played in New York following the attacks. The atmosphere was charged, with a feeling much like a World Series game. The Mets honored the fallen heroes from the New York police and fire departments by wearing helmets adorned with their initials. Diana Ross belted out "God Bless America" before the game, and Liza Minelli sang "New York, New York" during the 7th-inning stretch. And Mike Piazza capped the night with a tremendous, game-winning, two-run homer in the bottom of the eighth as the Mets topped the Braves 3–2.

Mike Piazza,
September 21, 2001

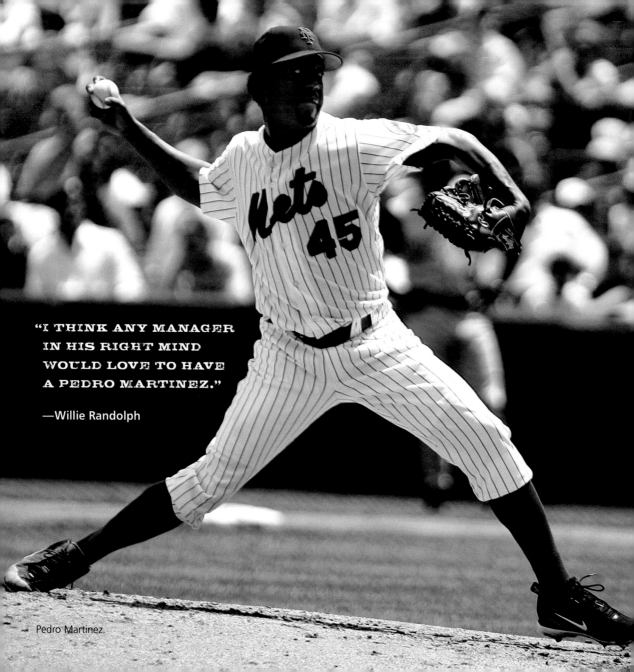

"I THINK ANY MANAGER
IN HIS RIGHT MIND
WOULD LOVE TO HAVE
A PEDRO MARTINEZ."

—Willie Randolph

Pedro Martinez.

91 Omar and Pedro

Mets GM Omar Minaya is good at getting what he wants. When he set out to rebuild the Mets in 2004, he set his sights on superstar pitcher Pedro Martinez, who had just helped the Boston Red Sox win their first World Series in 86 years. No biggie. Minaya simply fed Pedro's ego and offered him a bigger and longer contract than Boston did. Martinez decided to make the jump to the Mets, becoming the ace they sorely needed, and Minaya showed all of baseball that the Mets were serious about building a contender. It didn't take long. The Mets ran away with the NL's Eastern Division in 2006, and they fell just short of a trip to the World Series, losing to St. Louis in seven games in the NLCS. And in 2007, in his first start with the Mets after nearly a year on the disabled list recuperating from rotator cuff surgery, Pedro recorded his 3,000th strikeout, making him just the 15th pitcher in major-league history to reach that plateau.

Omar Minaya and Pedro Martinez

"I'M NOT THINKING ABOUT
OTHER TEAMS OR WHAT
PEOPLE THINK ABOUT
WHAT WE'RE DOING,
I'M JUST TRYING
TO WIN GAMES."

—Willie Randolph

92 Willie Randolph

Randolph left the Yankees' pinstripes for the Mets' orange and blue in 2004. The former Yankee second baseman and longtime coach finally got his chance to manage when Mets GM Omar Minaya chose him to succeed Art Howe. Randolph's 2005 Mets were competitive, making a run at the NL wild card, but his 2006 team was the best the Mets had fielded in a couple of decades. Randolph was at the helm as the Mets won 97 games and ended the Braves' streak of consecutive division titles at 14. Had star pitchers Pedro Martinez and Orlando Hernandez not gone down with injuries late in the season, the Mets most likely would have returned to the World Series for the first time since 2000. They fell just short, as the Cardinals' Yadier Molina stroked a ninth-inning two-run homer for a 3–1 win in Game 7 of the NLCS.

93 Lucky 7

The Mets set a team record for homers in a game on April 19, 2005, when they hit seven in a 16–4 pasting of the Philadelphia Phillies. Jose Reyes and Victor Diaz each hit two, and David Wright, Mike Piazza, and Doug Mientkiewicz added the others.

Paul Lo Duca tags out
Jeff Kent in Game 1
of the 2006 NLDS

94 Double Take

In the second inning of Game 1 of the 2006 NLDS at Shea Stadium, the Los Angeles Dodgers had two on and none out. Russell Martin hit a line drive to right field. Jeff Kent waited at second base to tag up, but J. D. Drew left first base immediately. The ball sailed over Shawn Green's head, and Kent took off. He was waved around third and sped for home. Mets catcher Paul Lo Duca snagged Jose Valentin's relay throw and tagged Kent out at the plate. Drew, close on Kent's heels and thinking he had also been waved home, slid in right behind Kent. Lo Duca, spotting Drew at the last second, also managed to tag Drew for an unbelievable double play. The Mets went on to win the game, 6–5.

95 Citi Field

Scheduled to open in 2009, the Mets' new home, Citi Field, will hold approximately 45,000 fans, with a natural grass field, an open-air environment, and a facade reminiscent of Brooklyn's Ebbets Field. The stadium will have seats oriented toward the infield to enhance sight lines, with more than 40 percent located on the lowest seating level, closer to the field. The asymmetrical layout should prove friendly to pitchers, with dimensions of 335 feet down the left-field line, 330 feet in right, and a hefty 408 feet to straightaway center field.

"A SUPERMAN CATCH."

— David Wright

96 Endy's Catch

Game 7 of the 2006 NLCS. The score was tied at 1. Mets starter Oliver Perez had just walked the Cardinals' Jim Edmonds, bringing up Scott Rolen with one out in the sixth inning. Rolen ripped Perez' first pitch toward the Cardinal bullpen in left field. Endy Chavez, replacing injured regular Cliff Floyd, took off after Rolen's rocket. As he reached the warning track in a dead sprint, Chavez leaped as high as his legs could take him. He stretched his glove well above the eight-foot fence, snagging the ball in the tip of the webbing, a classic ice-cream-cone catch. Unsure he had held on to the ball, Chavez first confirmed the spectacular catch, then wheeled and fired to second base for the relay to double up Edmonds at first. It stands as one of the greatest catches in post-season history.

97 Reyes of Hope

Jose Reyes is the man that gets things started. The speedy shortstop with a quick bat is a nightmare for opposing pitchers, who dread seeing him reach base. Reyes can wreak havoc once there, by disrupting the pitcher's concentration and routine. After struggling with injuries and a position change in his first few seasons with the Mets, Reyes really started to come into his own in 2006 when he batted .300 and stole a team-record 64 bases. He then broke his own record in 2007 when he stole 78 bases. Reyes is the first player in New York baseball history—including the Yankees, Giants, and Dodgers—ever to steal 50 or more bases in three straight years. In just five seasons, Reyes is already second in total stolen bases with the Mets, trailing only Mookie Wilson. He's considered one of the best all-around players in baseball today.

"WHEN YOU HAVE SPEED, YOU HAVE TO PUT THE PRESSURE ON THE OTHER TEAM. THAT'S WHAT I TRY TO DO ALL THE TIME."

—Jose Reyes

David Wright

98 All Wright!

With the arrival of David Wright, the Mets finally have the third baseman they've been seeking for more than 40 years. Wright is an excellent all-around player with the skills and power to become a superstar. He socked 27 home runs and drove in 102 runs in 2005, his first full season in the big leagues, and he hammered 26 homers to go with 116 RBI in 2006. In 2007, Wright put together an even better season, hitting .325 with 30 home runs, 107 RBI, and 34 stolen bases. At the 2006 All-Star Game, Wright slugged an astounding 16 homers in the first round of the annual home-run derby, ultimately finishing second in the three-round contest, to Philadelphia's Ryan Howard.

"HE'S THE COMPLETE PACKAGE. HE USES THE WHOLE FIELD WITH POWER ALL OVER THE PLACE. DEFENSIVELY, HE MAKES ALL THE PLAYS."

—Howard Johnson

99 Billy the Kid

Billy Wagner joined the Mets in 2006 after impressive stints as the closer in Houston and Philadelphia. The hard-throwing lefty brought his blazing fastball and wicked slider to a promising Mets team looking for late-inning dependability. His 31 consecutive saves over the course of the 2006 and 2007 seasons did just that, helping the Mets return to the playoffs in 2006.

100 Another Terrific Tom

With his win in the Mets' 8–3 victory over the Cubs on August 5, 2007, Tom Glavine became the 23rd pitcher in major-league history to win 300 games—and only the fifth lefty to ever reach the milestone. He's also the first to do it in a Mets uniform. It capped a remarkable weekend in baseball, following Barry Bond's 755th home run, which tied him with Hank Aaron for the all-time lead, and Alex Rodriguez' 500th homer, which made him the youngest ever to reach that plateau.

"I KNOW THE COMPANY I'M IN, AND I'M AS PROUD AS CAN BE TO BE IN THAT COMPANY."

—Tom Glavine

Tom Glavine during his 300th win

101 Mets Magic

Seven post-season appearances: 1969, 1973, 1986, 1988, 1999, 2000, and 2006; four National League pennants: 1969, 1973, 1986, and 2000; and the Miracles of 1969 and 1986.

Ray Knight celebrating his home run
in Game 7 of the 1986 World Series

Paul Lo Duca

Acknowledgments

It's hard for me to believe that this is the fourth book I've authored in this wonderful "101" series. Growing up with dreams of becoming an architect, and now primarily a graphic designer, I never imagined I would call myself an author. But I guess I am.

For providing me with this wonderful opportunity, a million thanks to my friend and mentor, Mary Tiegreen, and her husband, Hubert Pedroli, my golf buddy.

To my father, Ron Green Sr., and my brother, Ron Jr., thanks for the inspiration and guidance. You're the two best writers I know. Everyone should have the pleasure of reading your commentaries on sports and life on a daily basis.

To my team — they are treasures I truly cherish — my beautiful and ever-supportive wife, Mary; gorgeous and amazingly talented daughter, Savannah; handsome and brilliant son, Dakota; and good pal Sam, the dog, who slumbers through the not-so-occasional epithets I hurl at my computer; as I said last time, you're the best.

To the rest of my family — Ron, Mary, Walt, Teresa, Lindsay, Taylor, Mike, Wendy, Ryan, Jake, Maggie, Marcia, Jeff, Beth, Tamera, Molly, Edie, John, Maddie, and Jake — we are truly blessed. Thank you for your continuing love and support.

A special word of thanks goes out to Ted Ciuzio at AP Images. "Ready Teddy," as I like to call him, greets every new research challenge with amazing enthusiasm. And a big thank you to Laura Wulf, who provided an image of the Colorado Silver Bullets' Shannan Mitchem, when neither the AP nor the Hall of Fame could.

Lastly, to all the folks at Stewart, Tabori & Chang who had a hand in producing this book — specifically Jennifer Levesque and Leslie Stoker — many, many thanks for all your effort and support. You make it too enjoyable to be called work. And to Richard Slovak, our copy editor extraordinaire, we couldn't do it without you.

A Tiegreen Book

Published in 2008 by Stewart, Tabori & Chang
An imprint of Harry N. Abrams, Inc.

Library of Congress Cataloging-in-Publication Data

Green, David, 1959-
  101 reasons to love the Mets /
by David Green.
    p. cm.
    ISBN 978-1-58479-669-5
  1. New York Mets (Baseball team)—Miscellanea. I. Title.
    II. Title: One hundred one reasons to love the Mets.
    III. Title: One hundred and one reasons to love the Mets.

GV875.N45G74 2008
796.35709747'1—dc22
2007032571

Text copyright © 2008 David Green
Compilation copyright © 2008 Mary Tiegreen

Editor: Jennifer Levesque
Designer: David Green, Brightgreen Design
Production Manager: Jacquie Poirier

101 Reasons to Love the Mets is a book in the 101 REASONS TO LOVE™ series.

101 REASONS TO LOVE™ is a trademark of Mary Tiegreen and Hubert Pedroli.

Printed and bound in China
10 9 8 7 6 5 4 3 2 1

HNA ▮▮▮▮▮
harry n. abrams, inc.
a subsidiary of La Martinière Groupe

115 West 18th Street
New York, NY 10011
www.hnabooks.com

Photo Credits

Pages 1, 2-3, 6 (inset), 7, 8, 9, 10, 13, 15, 17, 18, 20, 21, 22, 26, 27 (inset), 28, 30-31, 34, 36, 37, 38, 40, 43, 44 (inset), 45, 46, 46 (inset), 49, 50, 51 (inset), 52, 53 (inset), 54, 56, 57, 58, 60, 62, 63 (inset), 64 (inset), 65, 66 (inset), 67, 68, 70, 71 (inset), 73, 75, 76, 78, 79 (inset), 80, 81 (inset), 82 (inset), 83, 84, 86-87, 88 (inset), 89, 91, 93, 94, 97, 98, 99 (inset), 101, 102, 103 (inset), 104, 106, 108-109, 110-111, 112, 115, 116-117, and 118 courtesy of AP Images.

Pages 5 (card), 11 (card), 12 (card), 16 (patch), 25, 29 (ball), 59 (ball), 32-33 (cards), 35 (card), 39 (pennant), 41 (card), 48 (card), 61 (ball), 74 (button), and 120 (ball) courtesy of David Green, Brightgreen Design.

Page 85 (inset) courtesy of Laura Wulf, Light Years Photography.